GETTING TO GRIPS WITH GOD'S WORD
A Series of Letters on Bible Study

Getting to Grips with God's Word

A SERIES OF LETTERS ON BIBLE STUDY

DAVID J NEWELL

JOHN RITCHIE LTD
CHRISTIAN PUBLICATIONS

40 Beansburn, Kilmarnock, Scotland

ISBN-13: 978 1 907731 23 5

Copyright © 2010 by John Ritchie Ltd.
40 Beansburn, Kilmarnock, Scotland

www.ritchiechristianmedia.co.uk

All rights reserved. No part of this publication may be reproduced, stored in a retrievable system, or transmitted in any form or by any other means – electronic, mechanical, photocopy, recording or otherwise – without prior permission of the copyright owner.

Typeset by John Ritchie Ltd., Kilmarnock
Printed by Bell & Bain Ltd., Glasgow

Contents

Preface 9

Letter No. 1 – The Basic Tools 11

Letter No. 2 – The Correct Attitude 17

Letter No. 3 – Getting an Overview 23

Letter No. 4 – Recognising the Genres 29

Letter No. 5 – Studying an Epistle 35

Letter No. 6 – Studying a Paragraph 41

Letter No. 7 – Studying Narrative (i) 47

Letter No. 8 – Studying Narrative (ii) 53

Letter No. 9 – Studying Bible Poetry 59

Letter No. 10 – Studying a Poem 65

Letter No. 11 – Studying a Parable 69

Letter No. 12 – Studying a Character 75

For John and Phillip

Preface

> Precious Bible! what a treasure
> Does the word of God afford?
> All I want for life or pleasure,
> Food and medicine, shield and sword:
> Let the world account me poor,
> Having this I need no more.
> (John Newton)

A few years ago a young friend asked for some help in studying his Bible. In response I wrote him a series of twelve letters which were later slightly revised and printed in *The Believer's Magazine*. They are now made available in a more permanent format in the hope that they will encourage young Christians to invest their time in the most exciting, challenging and rewarding of exercises – the serious investigation of God's inspired word.

David J Newell

Letter No. 1 – The Basic Tools

Dear John

    I am glad you want to learn how to study the scriptures, for there is nothing of greater importance to a believer. One of the results of regeneration (and therefore an evidence that we really are saved) is an in-built desire to read the word of God. After all, it is the food of the believer's new life: just as we have to eat physically to maintain our bodies so we must set aside time regularly to take in the spiritual nourishment of the word of God. Peter's instruction is clear enough: 'As newborn babes, desire the sincere milk of the word, that ye may grow thereby' (1 Pet 2.2). So let me set out the basic essentials.

    Any serious task requires tools, and the first tool of Bible study is **a reliable edition of the Bible**. Although written originally in Hebrew and Aramaic (the Old Testament), and Greek (the New Testament), the Bible loses little in translation. But it is imperative to use an accurate word for word rendering rather than one which simply attempts to communicate broad ideas by means of paraphrase or dynamic equivalence. May I suggest that there are two good reasons for staying with the King James Version of 1611. First, the King James Version attempts to translate precisely. When Paul writes that 'we [the apostles] speak, not in the words which man's wisdom teacheth, but which the Holy Ghost teacheth' (1 Cor 2.13), he is underlining the truth of verbal inspiration. That is to say, the individual words of scripture, not just the general concepts, are chosen by the Holy Spirit. Only a literal translation will do justice to those words. Thus, while my NIV renders Matthew 18.20 as 'For where two or three come together in my name, there am I with them', the KJV's 'For where two or three are gathered together in my name, there am I in the midst of them', is closer to the original. There is a big difference between the Lord Jesus merely being 'with' His gathered people and being in their 'midst' (a slightly archaic word for middle or centre). When believers gather to His name, the Saviour is not on the edge but at the very heart of the company.

Literal translation will sometimes bring puzzling Middle Eastern idioms over into English, but we can usually discover what they mean by investigating their use in other parts of scripture. Try, for example, Acts 9.28: 'And he [Paul] was with them <u>coming in and going out</u> at Jerusalem'. To understand that odd phrase, look at the similar language of Numbers 27.17, 2 Samuel 5.2, 1 Kings 3.7, Psalms 121.8 and 139.2. Those references, by the way, come from the *Treasury of Scripture Knowledge* (a wonderful compendium of marginal references and parallel passages) included in e-Sword. Better to do this work for yourself, and learn a great deal in the process, than surrender to the possibly inaccurate efforts of paraphrasers.

The second reason is that all the great commentaries of the past (for example, Matthew Henry, John Gill, Matthew Poole, Albert Barnes, C H Spurgeon, Jamieson Fausset and Brown, J N Darby) and Bible aids (Strong's and Young's concordances, Wigram's Englishman's Greek and Hebrew concordances) are based upon the KJV. Little of earth-shattering value has been written in the late twentieth and twenty-first centuries, for the riches of scripture have already been thoroughly mined by generations of Bible-loving scholars. You can afford to forgo the superficial, experience-centred paperbacks of today, but do not miss out on godly expositors of the past.

A particularly valuable edition of the KJV is Newberry's. This provides crisp paragraph headings, an excellent system of marginal references, alternative translations, and linguistic annotations which open up some of the more obscure details of God's word. Newberry's Bible itself went through several different editions, but the one to get (if you can) is the final, handy sized version. It includes a brief but clear introduction explaining the meaning of the annotations and the other special features.

It is also worth purchasing a cheap KJV (scour the charity shops) just for personal marking purposes. It is good to annotate your Bible because only as we write do we really learn. But discovering how to mark efficiently and intelligently takes practice. As a student I purchased a Cambridge wide-margin Bible and started assiduously cluttering the edges with what I thought were useful notes. Time proved how wrong I was. Instead, it is far better to use an old Bible to experiment with coloured underlining, highlighting, marginal notes and 'railway lines' (thin ink lines linking significant words and phrases on the same page). That way you will not ruin an expensive book. Some people like to Xerox a double-page spread from their usual Bible and use that for marking. A trip to your local stationers will equip you with a range of micro-tipped coloured marking pens. The great thing is to look closely, carefully and constantly at the text of scripture, and notice what you see.

Although it is wise to stick to one reliable translation as the basis for your study, there is much to be said for comparing it at times with others. William Tyndale's wonderful New Testament (1526 and 1534) is now readily available and will startle you with its freshness and clarity. In fact, most of the KJV New Testament is based upon his pioneering work. Others worth having on your shelf include the Revised Version of 1881, J N Darby's one-man translation (with its immensely valuable footnotes), and the New American Standard Bible. Remember: no translation is itself inspired or infallible, and therefore it is prudent to compare and contrast.

The second tool is **a sturdy notebook**. Marking one's Bible and writing out study notes are very different activities. Indeed, the first will usually be the considered result of the second. Joshua learned in Exodus 17.14 (the first allusion in scripture to a book) that what we write down we retain in our heads: 'And the LORD said unto Moses, Write this *for* a memorial in a book, and rehearse *it* in the ears of Joshua: for I will utterly put out the remembrance of Amalek from under heaven.' Bur whatever you do, do not resort to loose sheets of paper because you will lose them. I well remember my father, trained by the Second World War to conserve paper, using for his Bible notes the backs of old envelopes, advertising sheets, and any other odd scraps he could lay hold of. Then he would stuff them all inside his Bible, thus ensuring that the binding split. Instead, get hold of some hard-back notebooks which will last, and either use them in a simple consecutive way (writing up and dating your notes in journal style as you go through the scriptures), or label them for different biblical subjects. You might, for example, set aside one notebook for the Old Testament, one for the New Testament, one each for topical studies (Christology, ecclesiology, eschatology), and so on. I have found large sheets of A3 paper most valuable for sketching out thoughts, ideas and outlines, since the size allows space to link up, blot out and revise. But this is perhaps more useful for preparing messages than for the discipline of personal Bible study.

The third essential is **a regular time slot**. There is no point waiting until you have spare time because you never will. That is why Paul exhorts us to make the best use of every opportunity, 'redeeming the time, because the days are evil' (Eph 5.16). Therefore, bearing in mind your responsibilities, set aside a regular stretch of time once a week in which you can be quiet, alone and concentrate on your study. It might be early on a Saturday morning before the rest of the family is up and around. It may be during the time that other family members have to be out. You alone know your own timetable and can place your Bible study spot accordingly. But it *must* be a regular appointment; otherwise the whole point of study is lost. Study implies a systematic, regular, disciplined application to a subject. It is *not* the same as daily Bible reading: *that* is our daily bread, for 'man shall not live by bread alone, but by every word that proceedeth out of the mouth of God' (Matt 4.4). Study, on the other hand, is making time to get to grips with the details of the word, taking notes, looking up related passages, trying to grasp the development of a Bible chapter. Thus the Bereans proved their worth by searching (and the word implies hard work, meaning 'to investigate, examine, enquire into, scrutinise, sift, question') the scriptures daily, to check up on the teaching of Paul the apostle (Acts 17.11).

The fourth essential is **a sane plan of action**. There is no point sitting at a desk with half a dozen Bibles and ten commentaries lined up in front of you. The best stocked biblical library in the world is of no avail until you know how to use it. You see, you cannot study haphazardly. It demands careful organisation and clear goals. Decide whether you intend to investigate a book of the Bible or a topic. I recommend the former, since you cannot really attempt the latter until you have a good grasp of the individual books of the Bible. Philippians or 1 Thessalonians might be a good start, as they are both short and comparatively straightforward. Read through the entire book several times, jotting down your initial reactions. Ask yourself questions: what is the book basically about? to whom is it written? what are its key words? why is Paul writing? what sort of things is he teaching? Set yourself a task and stick at it. Remember: Bible study requires solid discipline and determination. We only get out of it what we can be bothered to put in. If we believe there is eternal benefit in getting to know God's word, we shall make every effort to stay the course. It will be tough, other duties and pleasures will intrude, you will become tired, Satan will try to discourage you – but just keep on!

The fifth essential is a clear understanding of **the ultimate aim of Bible study**. It is not so that we can beat our friends in Bible quizzes, or prepare sermons to dazzle the saints. Rather, it is that we might be spiritually fed and transformed. We study the word so that God might mould our lives for His glory. Never forget Paul's vital affirmation: 'All scripture *is* given by inspiration of God, and *is* profitable for doctrine, for reproof, for correction, for instruction in righteousness: that the man of God may be perfect, thoroughly furnished unto all good works' (2 Tim 3.16). Scripture aims to teach, warn, correct, and lead us in the right ways so that we might be complete, equipped for all the good works God desires of His people. Read Psalm 119 and find the nine times the psalmist asks God to 'teach me'. That should be the prayer of every Bible student.

May the Lord help you as you establish good habits for a lifetime.

Affectionately in Christ Jesus.

Letter No. 2 – The Correct Attitude

Dear John

Last time I wrote I listed some of the basic tools for successful Bible study. Now I want to talk about something rather more intangible but equally indispensable: the right condition of soul. Tools are useless without the necessary skill to use them effectively. The Bible, you see, is like any other book in that it needs to be read from beginning to end (and how few believers actually do that!), but it is also like no other book in that it requires a submissiveness of spirit if we want to unlock its riches. Come to the scripture with a critical arrogance and it will remain a closed volume. Come humbly with a reverential recognition that this is the very voice of God, and we shall find it having an impact upon our lives.

Psalm 119 is the greatest poem ever written about the value of God's word. Whoever wrote it (and it remains as tantalisingly but resolutely anonymous as the letter to the Hebrews), he was a man overwhelmed by the power of scripture. And remember that his Bible was probably simply the Pentateuch; hence his frequent references to 'the law'. How much greater is the privilege of believers today who have the entire revelation of God between two covers – not just the five books of Moses, but poetry, prophecy, gospel narrative, early church history, and doctrinal letters! Nevertheless, despite the narrowness of the canon available to him, the psalmist teaches us how to read scripture.

First, he insists that we LEARN (Psa 119.7,71,73). Scripture is not like the ephemeral literature of the 21st century – newspapers, magazines, passing best-sellers. These we read and forget almost at once. But the unchanging truth of God is to be stored in the treasure-house of our hearts. It is an education for life. Second, the repetition of his key word 'keep' and its synonyms urges us to OBEY what we read (Psa 119.2,4,5,8). There is no better way to learn than to obey. Even modern educationalists recognise that hands-on instruction has a more powerful impact than mere rote learning. The Lord Jesus, for example, commanded His people to remember Him at the breaking of bread, a truth that only comes alive as we put it into practice. Third, the psalmist counsels us to VENERATE the word, for it merits our 'respect' and 'fear' (Psa 119.15,38,63,120). King Josiah is a marvellous model: that young man was overcome with grief on discovering how far his nation had departed from God's commandments (2 Chron 34.19-21). He took seriously what he read. Our sorrow today, of course, will be reserved not so much for our nation or even our assembly but for our own failures. And finally the psalmist encourages us to ENJOY God's word (Psa 119.162; you might like to compare Job 23.12; Psalm 19.7-10; Jeremiah 15.16), for Bible study is not to be a drudgery but a delight. The book is, after all, like food, specifically like honey in its sweetness. It is also an invaluable treasure. The seventeenth-century poet George Herbert puts it like this:

> Oh Book! infinite sweetness! let my heart
> Suck every letter, and a honey gain,
> Precious for any grief in any part;
> To clear the breast, to mollify all pain.

The initial letters of my four key words (learn, obey, venerate and enjoy) spell out another: love (Psa 119.97). That, at root, must be our attitude to the Bible: 'O how I love thy law!'

What we love we tend to think about. That, so they tell me, is the common experience of human romance. Similarly, a love for God's word will issue in spiritual meditation, which simply means that we contemplate, ponder, and chew over the scriptures in our mind. This will lead to an increasing respect for the Bible's unity. No verse in this book stands in isolation. It is first of all part of a whole paragraph (so we should always look at verses in their immediate context). It is secondly part of a library so tightly unified that Genesis, for example, can unlock some of the mysteries of the Book of Revelation and *vice-versa*. The great value of getting the word into our heart and thinking about it is that we shall inevitably find other passages springing to mind and illuminating our understanding. It is Herbert again who makes the point:

> This verse marks that, and both do make a motion
> Unto a third, that ten leaves off doth lie.

In other words, in our study of scripture we shall constantly be coming across unexpected links and connections. That is the great boon of possessing a Bible packed with good marginal references. Every one of them will alert us to parallel passages, comparisons, contrasts, related verses and doctrines – all of which will shed light on our reading and help to make scripture plain. One of the many blessings of the Choice Gleanings yearly reading plan is that it disciplines us to confront three sections of the word daily: two from the Old Testament and one from the New. The result is that distant parts of the scriptures will be found often to complement and clarify one another.

Now, as I mentioned in my first letter, the whole aim of this is primarily to mould my life for God. Bible study must therefore have a serious input into my own spiritual development. It does not matter how accurately a young man can chart out the prophetic future as taught in the scriptures if he is, say, currently engaged in disobeying his parents. Lip service and head knowledge, all too often the great failing of believers raised in New Testament assemblies, are no substitute for reality of soul and earnest devotedness of life.

It is therefore sometimes useful to ask yourself three questions when you study a passage. **First, what is there here for my head to grasp?** Biblical truth is never to be divorced from the intelligence – rather, it is designed to fill and shape our entire mind-set for God. Throughout the word the living God is teaching us about Himself, about His programme for Israel, the church, and the world, about the glories of His Son, about the standards of living He expects of His redeemed people. Nothing fills and satisfies the mind like the word. **Second, what is there here for my heart to enjoy?** Unlike academic textbooks, which may stock the brainpan but never touch the heart, God's word warms the soul. It assures me of the Lord's unchanging love for His own, of His power to keep for ever all who have come to Him by faith, of the certainty of His soon return to take His saved people home to glory. It teaches me to view every circumstance in life as coming from the hands of an omnipotent God who works everything after the counsel of His own will (Eph 1.11). The Christian may not have an easy pathway down here (far from it), but he can be assured that all is ordained of God for his ultimate blessing. **Third, what is there here for my hands to do?** Doctrine and devotion are essential aspects of the word, but so is duty. Since God created us with a mind to think, emotions to be stirred, and a body through which to demonstrate practical obedience, it is hardly surprising that His word should challenge every part. Paul's great letter to the Ephesians falls into two sections: the first three chapters inform us of what God has done for His people, and the final three chapters instruct us as to how we should respond in daily obedience. Thus, a clear statement of doctrine leads into the obligation of duty. Our society, so blinded by the dead-end philosophy of instant pleasure and personal gain, has completely forgotten the stupendous benefits of duty. Duty makes life worth while. That God should entrust His people with the responsibility of living for Him in a rebel world is a privilege in itself. It gives a structure to our lives (which should of course revolve around the activities of the local assembly in which He has placed us), a motivation to see us through the dullest daily routines, and the consciousness of bringing Him pleasure.

In conclusion I cannot resist quoting Herbert again:

> Teach me, my God and King,
> In all things thee to see,
> And what I do in any thing,
> To do it as for thee:
>
> A servant with this clause
> Makes drudgery divine:
> Who sweeps a room, as for thy laws,
> Makes that and th'action fine.

Letter No. 2 – The Correct Attitude

May our reading and study of the word make us better people for God.

Affectionately in Christ Jesus

Letter No. 3 – Getting an Overview

Dear John

Having outlined the necessary tools and attitude of heart required for the effective study of God's word, it is now time to get a broad overview of the Bible as a whole. It is, after all, a big book which can easily daunt the reader. Indeed, it is best seen as a library of 66 different books, written over some 1500 years by about 40 different writers from a variety of backgrounds and countries. It includes, for example, legislation, historical narrative, biography, poetry, doctrinal and personal letters, architectural descriptions and predictive prophecy. The very fact that so many distinct books over such a period of time have one predominating theme is a testimony to the one great author – God Himself. Nothing else can explain the amazing coherence of scripture.

The best way to get a grasp of what we may call the Big Picture is to recognise that the books of the Bible fall into clear groupings. The pattern in the Old Testament is quite memorable in itself:

Old Testament
Pentateuch (5)   )   17
Historical Books (12))
Poetry (5)   5
Major Prophets (5))
Minor Prophets (12))   <u>17</u>
                                39 books

New Testament
Historical Books (5)   5
Letters (21)   21
Prophecy (1)   <u>1</u>
                                27 books

First of all we have the **Pentateuch** (the 5 books of Moses), which gives an historical survey stretching from the creation of the universe (Gen 1-2) to the arrival of the Israelites on the border of the promised land. The history of mankind from Adam to Abraham is squeezed into a mere 12 chapters; thereafter it is the people of Israel who take centre stage, because God formed them to be His special representatives in a sin-darkened world. There follow 12 **Historical Books** charting the rise and decline of Israel's kingdom under Saul, David and his successors, the division of that kingdom into north and south, and the final captivity of both parts because of disobedience. Then come 5 books of **Poetry**, ranging from Job's universally relevant examination of suffering and the psalmists' poems of lament and praise, to the pithy practical wisdom of Solomon, his analysis of the failure of man apart from God, and his love song celebrating the joys of marriage. The 5 **Major Prophets** candidly highlight Israel's spiritual failures as the cause of her captivity, while the 12 **Minor Prophets** (a title which merely indicates comparative size, not importance), covering a long period from the kingdom to the return from exile, continue to call the nation to repentance. One of the valuable exercises you can undertake is to see how the prophetic books fit into Israel's history. This is usually made plain in the introductory verses, which name the kings who were reigning when the prophet wrote. Those Minor Prophets become much more interesting and intelligible when we place them in their proper context. Amid the darkest times they courageously called the people back to God. Yet, through all the gloom of Israel's moral and spiritual breakdown, shines the sure hope of the coming of a great Deliverer who would never fail but would redeem His people and establish a righteous reign over the entire world. The whole Old Testament resounds with the message, 'Behold, he shall come' (Mal 3.1). And this coming Saviour, described as the Messiah (which simply means 'the anointed one'), would be the ultimate prophet (fully revealing God to His creatures), priest (finally dealing with sin) and king (governing in righteousness).

After the 400 or so year gap which follows the conclusion of the Old Testament a new note is struck. Matthew introduces his gospel as 'the book of the generation of Jesus Christ [which is simply the New Testament equivalent of "Messiah"], the son of David, the son of Abraham'. The language sets up a deliberate parallel with the first book of the Old Testament by echoing the structural formulae of Genesis ('these are the generations of'). Further, Matthew's gospel presents the Lord Jesus as the fulfilment of God's special covenant promises to David (recorded in 2 Samuel 7.12-16) and to Abraham (recorded in Genesis 12.1-3). The Lord Jesus Christ is therefore both the long-expected king of Israel *and* the bringer of blessing to all nations. All God's purposes find their fulfilment in Him. The rest of the New Testament elaborates on this truth. The 5 **Historical Books** provide four complementary accounts of the Lord's public ministry (with different emphases, so that Matthew highlights His kingship, Mark His service, Luke His manhood and John His deity) which run on into a record of the evangelistic activities of the early believers. Once the Lord Jesus had ascended back to heaven, they began, after the day of Pentecost, spreading the good news so that the message spilt beyond Israel into the whole world. After this historical foundation comes a series of 21 doctrinal **Letters** which explain the significance of the work of Christ, the lifestyle expected of Christian believers, the way in which God's people are to gather for worship and service, and the sure hope of the Lord's coming again for His people. And the capstone is the New Testament's one book of **Prophecy,** which takes the wraps off future events by intimating the Saviour's coming triumph, entitled, significantly, the book of Revelation.

One of the benefits of grasping this overview is that it enables us to slot any passage we are studying into the grand plan of scripture. If we are seeking clear statements of Christian doctrine we go first of all to the New Testament letters, in which the Holy Spirit reveals the mind of God for believers of this age (1 Tim 3.15). The gospels, you see, are inspired historical accounts of a unique period of time in which unrepeatable events took place. The Lord Jesus will never again be born, die and rise from the tomb. In Matthew 10 He sent out His disciples to preach specifically *not* to Gentiles but only to 'the lost sheep of the house of Israel', whereas in Matthew 28 He ordered the same men to reach out to the entire world. Which commission concerns us today? I know of no Christians who believe we should be obeying the first. Even the first part of the Acts records exceptional happenings when new believers assembled together in the Temple precincts at Jerusalem, when apostles worked extraordinary credential miracles, when saved Gentiles were only gradually accepted into companies of believers, when Paul still observed the Jewish feasts – details which signal a historical context which is for ever past. This is not to deny the abiding lessons, moral principles, and illustrations of God's dealings found in these books, but simply to recognise that they do not directly describe the age in which we live. In our era the Lord Jesus Christ is at God's right hand in heaven, the Holy Spirit indwells His people on earth, and God is taking out from the Gentiles a people for His name. Similarly, while the Old Testament was certainly written 'for our instruction' it was not written directly *to* us, but largely to a chosen nation called out for God, a nation given a code of law, a complex ritual of worship, and a geographical slice of land. There is much we can learn from Israel, but we do not belong to Israel. Rather, we belong to a heavenly company of people, the church, the body of Christ, and nothing but confusion is created when Bible readers fail to observe the distinction.

A great way of making sense of the Old Testament is to see how it **all points to the Saviour**. Never forget that although the eternal Son of God entered humanity historically at His incarnation, He did not begin His existence then. In Old Testament times He was fully active in creation (John 1.1-3), in revelation (John 1.18), and in salvation (John 5.17). Further, the very structure of Bible history is designed to testify to Him. In the Pentateuch, for example, we have Christ *foreshadowed* (in types like the Passover lamb, the brazen serpent, the smitten rock); in the poetical books we find Christ's *feelings* (read Psalms 22 and 69 especially); in the prophets we have Christ directly *foretold* (in the graphic details of Isaiah 53, so scrupulously fulfilled in His life and death, or the specific birth location announced in Micah 5.2). Someone has described the Old Testament as a beautiful but dimly lit room, the gorgeous contents of which cannot fully be seen and appreciated until bright light streams in from the New Testament. That is why it is often said that the New is in the Old concealed, while the Old is by the New revealed; or, if you prefer it, the New is in the Old contained, the Old is by the New explained. All the unexplained ceremonies, unfulfilled prophecies and unsatisfied longings of the Old Testament find their answer in the Lord Jesus Christ. Once we see this, the pieces of the jigsaw begin to fall into place. Just bear in mind that God is always first of all thinking of His Son. That being so, how important that *we* should endeavour to glimpse His glories in the word (Luke 24.27). To see Christ in all the scriptures will help shape our lives, guard our paths, and fill our hearts with praise when we gather to remember Him.

Affectionately in Christ Jesus

Letter No. 4 – Recognising the Genres

Dear John

Now you have gained an overview of scripture as a whole you are in a position to investigate individual books – always the best way to conduct your Bible study. One of my regrets is that as a young man I fell into the easy trap of squeezing the juice out of individual verses (often for the purpose of preaching the gospel or giving a little word of ministry) instead of seeking the sense of the whole book in which they were found. As a consequence, my study became random and desultory instead of systematic and methodical. One of the sadder characteristics of much assembly preaching is the tendency to construct gospel messages from three or four texts ripped out of context and pasted together. This implicitly propagates the false and indeed dangerous notion that you can make God's word mean whatever you want. I still recall nearly falling off my seat in amazement a few years ago on hearing one gospel preacher use Job 41.8 in his exhortation to the unsaved. The verse reads as follows: 'Lay thine hand upon him, remember the battle, do no more.' This, I was told, meant that the sinner should lay hold on Christ in faith, look back to the victory of Calvary, and cease from attempting salvation by good works. The doctrine, in terms of biblical soteriology, is correct enough, but it is not at all what the passage means. Read that verse in its context and you will see it is all about the inadvisability of messing around with leviathan, who was, I take it, a huge sea-going dinosaur. To do such violence to the face-value significance of scripture is to bring God's truth into discredit, for an intelligent listener will simply go away thinking that Christianity is so completely irrational that it is therefore beyond normal examination. Nothing could be further from the truth. Paul preached the gospel expecting his hearers to check his message against the specific teaching of the Old Testament (Acts 17.11). Never forget: God says what He means and means what He says. The

Bible is not a book of coded mysteries to be explained only by some professional elite. God graciously conforms to the conventional rules of human language and grammar.

Before getting into an individual book of scripture, however, we need some idea of the various literary genres used in the Bible. Within its substantial library of 66 books we find a wonderful variety of writing forms. It should come as no surprise that there is as much diversity and beauty in the written word as in the created world. In human writing we automatically distinguish between the language and style of a love-letter, a cake recipe, and a university thesis. The same writer will employ different techniques in each case, because each genre has a distinct aim in view. In the Bible three main genres stand out.

First of all, there is straightforward **narrative**. This covers the historical books of both testaments. The story of Israel's nationhood, the lives of its patriarchs and kings, the New Testament gospel records and Luke's summary of church history all constitute narrative. It may include, among other things, historical records, details of legislation, religious ceremony and architecture, biography, conversations, parables and sermons. If you are reading, say, the book of Genesis, you are confronted with an infallibly accurate but carefully selected record of ancient history uniquely organised by the Spirit of God so as to provide spiritual nourishment for believers today. Bible history is always more than mere history (1 Cor 10.11). You could watch out for four areas of significance. First there is the <u>historical progress</u> of God's people Israel from the calling out of their founding father Abraham in Genesis 12 to become the ancestor of the promised Messiah. God will always accomplish His purpose, despite the failings of His servants. Second, there are valuable <u>individual portraits</u> of men and women, good and bad, from which we can learn practical lessons in godliness. In Genesis, for example, there are seven great men worth careful study (Adam, Enoch, Noah, Abraham, Isaac, Jacob, Joseph). Third, there are clear <u>moral principles</u> demonstrated in God's dealings with men: He is seen as the God who creates, commands, calls, intervenes in judgment and provides salvation. Fourth, you might catch glimpses of Christ in the <u>typical pictures</u> that pepper the book. Typology refers to the way in which God has organised history and the inspired record of it in scripture so that it speaks in advance of the coming and the work of His beloved Son. Thus in Genesis we find several remarkable illustrations of Calvary: Adam's deep sleep whereby

Letter No. 4 – Recognising the Genres

God formed Eve out of his side (Gen 2.21-23); the coats of skin which clothed guilty Adam and Eve (Gen 3.21); the death of Abel as the victim of Cain's hatred (Gen 4.8); the sacrifices Noah offered after the flood, sacrifices which brought God delight (Gen 8.20-21); the giving of the only son Isaac in sacrifice on Moriah (Gen 22.2); the divinely provided substitute of the ram (Gen 22.13). Biblical narrative, whether in the Old or New Testament, is full of precious lessons about the goodness of God, the sinfulness of man, the inviolability of the divine purpose, and the centrality of the person and work of Christ.

Second, there is **poetry**. This comprehends the group of books at the centre of the Old Testament (Job, Psalms, Proverbs, Ecclesiastes, Song of Solomon) as well as most of the prophets, who delivered their oracles in poetic form. One of the great characteristics of poetry is its memorability: it strengthens expression and carves it on the mind through repetition and striking imagery. Unlike English verse, Hebrew poetry does not use repetition of sound (rhyme) or rhythm (metre), but reiterates ideas in parallel phrases. If you want to see the difference poetry makes, try reading the account of the death of General Sisera in Judges where it is recorded twice – once as prose narrative (Jud 4.17-21), and once as poetry in the colourful Song of Deborah (Jud 5.24-27). Again, compare the historical creation account in Genesis 1 - 2.4 with the poetry of Psalm 104. The book of Psalms consists of 150 marvellous inspired song lyrics of varying length and structure devoted to the praise of God, the record of human experiences of God's mercy, and the encouragement of God's people. Thus, instead of simply saying that true happiness comes through spiritual separation, the psalmist writes, 'Blessed *is* the man that walketh not in the counsel of the ungodly, nor standeth in the way of sinners, nor sitteth in the seat of the scornful.' (Psa 1.1) These three parallel phrases help us understand what ungodliness really is (sin and mockery of God), expose the insidious addictiveness of close association with the wicked (from casual walking and standing to sitting down in fixed fellowship), and highlight the pressures on the individual believer ('the man') in a world where 'sinners' (plural) are in the majority. It is tough to take a stand for God, but it is worth it. One of the great Reformers said that you can find a psalm to match every experience of life. Whether going though times of prosperity or penury, whether spiritually depressed or elated, there will be a psalm that meets your need and expresses the feelings of your heart before

God. Believers over the years have found this book an inexhaustible mine of spiritual comfort. But I shall return to this in greater detail in a later letter.

Let me say just a word about imagery. To recognise imagery in the Bible does not mean that one has departed from the principles of literal interpretation. On the contrary, to read any text in a natural way is to allow for and correctly interpret figures of speech (simile, metaphor, personification) just as one does routinely in daily life. No one believes that the man who in a crisis loses his head, or whose eyes pop out, or who is asked to lend an ear, is anatomically deprived. Such language arrests our attention and sticks in the mind. In the same way the psalmist speaks movingly of his sorrow: 'I am weary with my groaning; all the night make I my bed to swim; I water my couch with my tears' (Psa 6.6).

The final generic category is what I shall simply call **doctrine**. This comprehends all the New Testament letters in which the apostles teach the truth of God for believers of this dispensation directly, logically, rigorously and yet palatably. It is always doctrine in the context of Christian fellowship (for no believer is expected to be outside the local assembly), brotherly warmth, and practical living. Unlike academic treatises, the doctrinal books of the Bible are never cold, detached, clinical or abstract. Read in Philippians 2.5-11 Paul's wonderful account of the voluntary self-humbling and consequent exaltation of the Son of God and see how it is essentially part of a very practical passage on the necessity of lowliness among the Lord's people. Paul was writing to defuse potential division in an assembly where two of the women were at loggerheads (Phil 4.2). There was no better way to do it than to focus upon the grace of Christ Jesus. Or read Peter's great exposition of the value of Calvary in 1 Peter 3.18, and see how it fits into a section encouraging Christians who were going through extreme suffering because of their faith in the Lord Jesus. In the Bible doctrine is nothing if not dynamic. Of course, all Bible books contain doctrinal truth, but in the New Testament only the letters are devoted to its systematic exposition. That is why we find in them clear teaching as to how a local assembly should function, what the death of Christ means, how believers should behave in the world today, and what lies ahead for God's saints.

Don't be misled into thinking that doctrine is dull. I still occasionally hear people denigrating it in favour of what they call 'practical teaching'. But there can be no true practical godly living without the foundation of accurate doctrine. And doctrine, properly appreciated, will cheer your soul and feed your mind. Those who do not find their spirits lifted by the great doctrines of the faith are probably not saved.

Keep reading!

Affectionately in Christ Jesus

Letter No. 5 – Studying an Epistle

Dear John

It is now time to put learning into practice. There are, may I suggest, three procedures for investigating any book of the Bible.

1. Repeatedly read through the book, because the key rule for study is read, read, and read again!
2. Divide it into logical paragraph sections for analysis.
3. Study each section verse by verse on the **OIA** principle (**O**bserve what is there; **I**nterpret what it means; **A**pply it to your life).

There is just no substitute for this verse-by-verse analysis. But you must not lose sight of the wood for the trees, so it is important at the same time to have an overview of the whole book. Of course, an accurate overview is only possible after detailed study, but you can get a broad idea of a book by using the following five headings, suitable for any New Testament epistle: **Author** (who wrote it), **Background** (when, why, and to whom it was written), **Construction** (the structural pattern of the book), **Distinctives** (how it differs from other New Testament books) and **Encouragement** (why it is especially enjoyable and helpful for the believer). If you can apply this method to one letter you will be able to apply it to them all. What follows, then, is an approach to Paul's letter to the Ephesians.

A - AUTHOR
Look through the letter and jot down all the personal references to see what they tell us about the writer. When you have collected them, sort them methodically into headings or points. Here is a possible list, with some practical applications.

Clearly, Paul is the writer (1.1; 3.1). The first thing we note is his

apostleship (1.1). Paul had divinely-given apostolic credentials: he had seen the risen Christ (1 Cor 9.1), he had power to work sign miracles (2 Cor 12.12), and like all the apostles he taught with divine authority (2 Pet 3.2). This last means that *what Paul says, the Lord says* (1 Thess 4.15). To disobey his writings is to disobey the Lord. Further, he had a deep **concern** for the spiritual progress of God's people (Eph 1.15-17). May we be similarly interested in the welfare of believers. A man of steadfast **consistency**, he practised what he preached (1.16; 6.18), showing a moral as well as an apostolic authority. Nevertheless, **suffering** (3.1, 13; 4.1; 6.20) dogged his steps. Ephesians, like Philippians and Colossians, is one of the prison epistles, a product of Paul's Roman confinement for the sake of Christ. Paul's life proves that faithfulness to the Lord Jesus does not necessarily guarantee prosperity down here. Paul's **privilege** was to be specially entrusted with the revelation of God's secret about Christ and the Church (3.2-7). Yet he was marked by **humility** (3.8), glorying not in his attainment or wisdom but in God's grace to him (3.2,7,8). And humility produced **reverence** (3.14): his grasp of truth generated an attitude of awe. Those who know the scriptures best will fear God most. Although it seemed later as if there was little fruit to show for his time in Ephesus (2 Tim 1.15), the issue for Paul was not outward success but **faithfulness** to the divine commission (Eph 6.19-20). Whatever the results, we are to be true to God's word. Paul, however, did not despise the prayers of the saints; rather, sensing his own **dependence** (6.19), he coveted them. If an apostle needed prayer, how much more do we? Finally, Paul loved **fellowship** (6.21-22), and was happy to share his experiences with believers to keep them informed. The value of a local assembly is that it provides a sphere for sharing in the things of God.

B - BACKGROUND

Background sounds boring, but it can throw much light on the word. The book of Acts and a good Bible encyclopaedia will quickly illuminate the setting. Ephesus, the leading city of the Roman province of Asia, with an estimated population of around 250,000, was noted as a centre of **politics**; indeed, it seems to have been the *de facto* capital of the area. As the third or fourth greatest city in the New Testament world it was also a centre of **commerce**, situated on the River Cayster, 6 miles from the sea, but linked by a connecting channel. A centre of **religion**, it boasted the Temple of Diana or Artemis, with vast columns of marble overlaid with gold, one of the seven wonders of the world (Acts 19.24,35), long lost but rediscovered in 1869 under 20 feet of soil. Not surprisingly it was also a centre of **tourism** (19.24-29) with a thriving souvenir industry and a 25,000-seater theatre. It was therefore an ideal base for gospel work (19.10), for the early evangelists went to where needy people were.

Paul's Ephesian experience, recorded for us in Acts 19, is mirrored in the development of his letter. Believers are called out from the world by God's sovereign intervention (Acts 19.8-10; Eph 1-3), their conduct is influenced by their new life in Christ (Acts 19.18-20; Eph 4-5), and they inevitably face conflict with a hostile society (Acts 19.23-41; Eph 6). The assembly was instructed by Paul during a two-year stay, this foundational teaching being followed up later by his ministry to the elders (Acts 20.17-38), his prison epistle from Rome, and the sending of Timothy to continue their training (1 Tim 1.3). The sad final word comes in Revelation 2.1-7. Despite having more teaching than any other assembly in the New Testament, Ephesus is finally accused of having left its first love. Paul's solemn warning to the elders is therefore still relevant to us all (Acts 20.31-32). Whatever our privileges we must stand firm against doctrinal error, against spiritual complacency, against moral failure.

C - CONSTRUCTION

Every book has its own structural pattern. This one falls neatly into two parts:

Part 1   1.1 – 3.21 (ending with 'Amen')
Part 2   4.1 - 6.24 (again ending with 'Amen').

Part 1 is about what God has done for us (it is full of doctrine); Part 2 is about how we should live (it emphasises our duty). The connecting word 'therefore' (4.1) signals the shift from the first part to the second. This logical progression makes the point that just as daily behaviour must rest on the firm foundation of sound doctrine, so true doctrine must always result in godly conduct. You see, what I believe influences how I live. It is a sobering challenge: am I 'walking worthy' of God's high calling? (4.1)

Believers are described in three positions: we 'sit' (2.6), 'walk' (4.1), and 'stand' (6.14). As victors we sit (1.1 – 3.21). We are seated (a fact, not a command) with Christ in the heavenlies (1.20;

2.6) where He is enthroned in all the dignity of His finished work (Heb 1.3; 10.12; 12.2). This describes our blessings. As pilgrims we walk through a dark and dangerous world (4.1 – 6.9), for our responsibility is to live down here as those who belong to Christ. This describes our behaviour. As soldiers we stand (6.10-24), holding our God-given ground against the assaults of Satan. This describes our battles. While it is physically impossible to sit and walk and stand simultaneously, every believer is in the good of these truths: we rest in what Christ has done, we progress through a sinful world to glory, and we fight against spiritual wickedness.

D - DISTINCTIVES

Try counting key words to get an idea of the letter's major interests. For example, 'church' and 'body' both appear 9 times, 'grace' 12 times. Ephesians unfolds the unique **character of the universal church** (3.2-13), that vast company of believers formed at the Day of Pentecost and completed at the Lord's return. To indicate its dignity, Paul uses three illustrations. It is the body of Christ, animated by His life (1.22-23); it is a temple in the Lord, filled with His light (2.21); and it is His bride, the object of His love (5.22-33). The metaphor of 'one new man' (2.13-15) announces an entirely new work whereby saved Jews and Gentiles are joined together in equal blessing. The church in its universal aspect is a new, heavenly assembly of people, unheard of in the Old Testament, wholly one in Christ, and destined for glory. Could we be in better company? Second, Paul unveils the **comprehensiveness of God's purpose** (1.9-10) to glorify Himself in redeemed sinners, finally heading up all things in Christ. Believers alone know the ultimate goal of history! Third, we discover the astonishing **completeness of our blessing** (1.3-9), blessing which goes out in accordance with God's grace rather than our need. Fourth, we are given insight into the **conflict of the believer** with a Satanically-dominated world (6.10-20). Finally, we are reminded of the **contrast between what we were and what we are** (2.11). We were *dead* (2.1-3), but are now alive (2.4-7); we were *distant* (2.11-12), but are now made near (2.13-18); we were *defiled* (4.17-19), but now are holy (4.20-24); and we were *darkness*, but now are light in the Lord (5.8).

E - ENCOURAGEMENT

How is this letter especially valuable? By lifting us up into 'the heavenlies' (1.3) it is the divine antidote to depression, lethargy,

Letter No. 5 – Studying an Epistle

and irresponsibility. When you feel discouraged, read the first three chapters and become taken up with God's amazing programme of grace to rescue and ennoble helpless sinners. If that does not cheer you, nothing will! Ephesians reminds us that everything we have is 'in Christ' (try counting the occurrences of the phrase). He is the origin, the sphere, and the end of our blessings. No wonder Christians love to give Him the pre-eminence! Keep reading!

Affectionately in Christ Jesus

Letter No. 6 – Studying a Paragraph

Dear John

My last letter attempted to give you a brief survey of Paul's epistle to the Ephesians, just to make the point that it is tremendously useful to have some kind of overview in order to grasp the structural design of a book. Every Bible book has its own unique pattern. The parts only make proper sense in the light of the whole. It is like assembling a bookcase from the individual pieces contained in a flat pack: you need a picture or plan to help you see how each bit fits into the finished product. But with Bible study there is a striking difference: in order to get that necessary bird's eye view, one needs first to have studied the whole book in detail. Although a Bible teacher will probably start a ministry series on Ephesians with a telescopic introduction, that introduction is the result of detailed, microscopic verse by verse analysis. The best teachers write their introductory talks at the very conclusion of their studies!

Let us now see how to tackle the raw detail of Paul's letter. Our sample for purposes of analysis will be the first two sections of the first chapter. Read through the chapter as a whole and look for the paragraphs. All writing falls into logical sections, like the letter I am writing to you. I think you will find that there are three clear units of material in Ephesians 1. **First**, there is a formal opening to the letter (Eph 1.1-2). Whereas today we begin 'Dear John' and end with conventional (and fairly meaningless) greetings such as 'lots of love, Uncle David', New Testament letters include that information right at the start. **Second**, I think we might notice that Paul's list of the believer's blessings which begins in verse 3 stretches right through to the end of verse 14. **Third**, the rest of the chapter (1.15-23) is devoted to outlining Paul's comprehensive prayer on behalf of the Christians. Its first word, 'wherefore' (which merely means 'therefore'), indicates that what Paul is now writing follows on logically from what he has just penned. It is a good exercise to think up appropriate and memorable headings to sum up the main teaching of each paragraph. For example, we could call the first section **Prologue** (because it begins the letter); the second **Praise** (because Paul is blessing God for His goodness to us); and the third **Prayer** (because it records Paul's desire for the spiritual growth of the Ephesian Christians). Do not feel that you have to resort to alliteration's artful aid (as someone calls it), but apt, crisp captions can be handy.

Now let us get into the first paragraph (verses 1-2) in a little depth. Never overlook introductions.

> Paul, an apostle of Jesus Christ by the will of God, to the saints which are at Ephesus, and to the faithful in Christ Jesus:
> Grace *be* to you, and peace, from God our Father, and *from* the Lord Jesus Christ.

After jotting down who is writing and to whom, the <u>first thing</u> you can do is select some key words to look up in your concordance and Bible dictionary. There are five significant NOUNS here: apostle, saints, faithful, grace, peace. To find out what a New Testament word means we need to consult (i) a good concordance (Strong's, Young's or e-Sword) to see how the same Greek word is used elsewhere in the New Testament, and (ii) W E Vine's *Expository Dictionary* for incisive definitions (but make sure you are looking under the correct Greek word; this is easily done because most of the time Vine lists every occurrence). For example, look up 'apostle' in your concordance and you will find it translates *apostolos*, meaning 'messenger'. It appears 81 times in the New Testament. In fact in Philippians 2.25 it is used of Epaphroditus and translated 'messenger' in the KJV. See how many times the word refers to the twelve apostles of the Lord Jesus. Does it ever refer to anyone else? What were the qualifications of the Lord's apostles? Are there any apostles today? Your study of this word will provide you with interesting and practical results. For a start, you will learn that any cult or religious system which claims to have living apostles just like the Lord's is a fraud. Of course, once you have done the basic spade work, you will not need

Letter No. 6 – Studying a Paragraph

to do it again when the word reappears in other parts of the Bible. Bible study, you see, involves the continual building up of a database of spiritual information, all of which helps us as we read more of the word. That is why it is so necessary to keep a record of our study in a notebook, on our computer, or in the margins of our Bible.

The <u>second thing</u> you might do is look at the divine NAMES in this section: Jesus Christ, Christ Jesus, the Lord Jesus Christ, God, God our Father. Why does Paul speak of Christ in different ways? According to Paul, what do these divine persons do for us? Why do you think they are they mentioned so frequently in just two verses?

A <u>third thing</u> is to note the ORDER in which things appear. This can often be interesting and important. For example, grace comes before peace. Just a little thing, you say. But it spells out the whole basis upon which God blesses His people. You will already have discovered what grace means. And grace is the foundation plank of every spiritual blessing: we only enjoy peace with God because He has first of all acted towards us in kindness. To grasp this will encourage constant humility, assurance and thankfulness.

Having recorded our discoveries in the first two verses we can move on into the second paragraph of the chapter. You might like to think of it as a prose poem consisting of three stanzas, each ending with a refrain ascribing praise to God (1.6,12,14; notice that all three verses use the words 'praise' and 'glory'). This in itself answers the great question, 'Why ever did God choose to save *me,* of all people?' It was not because of my goodness but for the glory of His name. Our salvation magnifies God, for He did it all. Hence each stanza is devoted to the distinctive saving activity of one person of the Trinity.

First, what did the FATHER do for us? You will see some key words in verses 3-6: list them and look them up. It is worth noting that a Bible word may be used in different ways in different contexts. For example, Paul blesses God for blessing us. Look up what Vine says about this word. It means 'to speak well of someone'. We bless God by speaking about His excellencies as they are revealed to us in the word (1 Pet 2.9, JND). That is what praise is all about, which gives a clue as to what we should be doing at the breaking of bread meeting. God blesses us, on the other hand, by freely bestowing upon us wonderful benefits beyond our mind's ability to comprehend. Note carefully where and of what kind these blessings are. Paul is certainly

Getting to Grips with God's Word

not thinking of physical and material advantages, for not all believers enjoy health, wealth and a secure environment down here. The Saviour came to give His people 'life more abundant' (John 10.10), irrespective of earthly conditions. Paul was writing from the discomfort of a Roman prison, yet he was simultaneously enjoying his spiritual riches in the heavenlies. Whatever our earthly situation, our spiritual blessings are safe in Christ. Never forget that, for it marks the distinctive character of the church age. Israel's benefits were primarily earthly, ours heavenly. The Father's activity in this section might be summed up in the simple phrase 'He hath chosen us' (but notice where, when and why).

Second, what about the SON (verses 7-12)? Note that He is described as 'the Beloved' (v 6), and check Matthew 3.17 to find out what that means. List the blessings we have in Christ. Investigate the crucial Bible word 'blood', which refers in context here to the Saviour's sacrificial death, a death which satisfies God's heart and permits Him justly to pardon sinners like you and me. What is God's long-term goal (v 10)?

Third, the HOLY SPIRIT (verses 13-14) has sealed believers as God's exclusive property. To understand what a seal involves, do some concordance work in both the Old and New Testaments. You will find (I hope!) that it speaks of authority, security and ownership. How else is the Holy Spirit described in these two verses? 'Redemption' in verse 7 speaks of something we have now, whereas in verse 14 it looks to the future. Look up Romans 8.23: in what sense are we still waiting to be redeemed? What do you think 'the purchased possession' is?

Now all this involves considerable toil, looking up key words, jotting down important cross references, formulating careful conclusions from the biblical evidence. Proverbs 2.1-5 frankly spells out both the cost and the benefit of diligent study. Study will cut you off from much so-called 'Christian' socializing, and it may even antagonise those of your peers who have no real appetite for God's word. You may well find that you spend several weeks slowly working at just one paragraph. But do not give up, for it is worth all the effort. Bible study, remember, is a long-term investment. There is no gain without pain. At the end of working though Ephesians 1.1-14, you should have discovered, if nothing else, that salvation is so great that it

Letter No. 6 – Studying a Paragraph

required the cooperative participation of each person of the triune Godhead: the Father chose us, the Son redeemed us, and the Holy Spirit sealed us. We just cannot be safer!

Buckle down to it. Record your discoveries so that you can build upon them in the future, and always try to use what you have learned in your assembly worship and service. And may the Lord help you to stick at it.

Affectionately in Christ Jesus

Letter No. 7 – Studying Narrative (i)

Dear John

    I hope you have been able to follow what I have tried to say over the past few letters. Like many things, however, Bible study (as they put it in Scotland) is 'better felt than telt': you really begin to grasp what it is all about only as you do it. There can be no substitute for hands-on experience. The more you dig into the word the more you will feel at home with it. It is rather like studying poetry. I tell my students that they will only truly understand one poem after they have read many, which does not always cheer them up greatly because it implies hard work, but (as I have said before) there is no gain without pain.

    After our brief glance at Ephesians (a sample letter), we can move on to the study of New Testament narrative. This may seem initially more difficult than a letter for the simple reason that it does not communicate doctrine in a direct manner. Narrative, you see, means telling a story, yet that story can include many other things (songs, dialogue, scenic description). The first five books of the New Testament consist of narrative: four accounts of the earthly activities of the Lord Jesus Christ, and one survey of early church history up to Paul's first Roman imprisonment. We shall focus for the moment on one of the gospels. Now, the four gospels are packed with an amazing variety of literary forms, which makes them among the most readable and enjoyable of Bible books. They include, for example, genealogy (Matt 1; Luke 3), poetry (Luke 1.68-79), sermons (Matt 5-7), miracles (Mark 2.1-12), parables (Luke 15), personal interviews (John 3), racy dialogue (John 9), fast-moving action (John 18), and prophetic overviews (Matt 24-25).

    As I have already said, the immediate trouble with narrative is that it does not teach lessons in a direct and propositional manner. It is not a series of doctrinal statements or practical exhortations. Rather, it provides an inspired account of God's ways in human history. Paul's letter to the Ephesians, for example, tells us in no uncertain terms what to believe and how to behave, but Luke's gospel is a selective historical account of the earthly activities of the Saviour, designed to foster confidence among those who have trusted Him for salvation (Luke 1.1-4). Of course, any information about the Lord Jesus will strengthen our faith in Him, increase our love for Him, and influence our lives, but in a narrative the information is usually communicated without any attempt at direct application. Each reader has to draw out the implications of a passage for himself.

This will all, I hope, make sense as we get into some examples. Let us investigate Luke 4.16-30. First, put the paragraph in its context. Never forget the **contextual location** of the section of narrative you are studying. Bible chapters and verses are not free-floating gobbets of information to be interpreted or used as the fancy takes you, but are always locked into a precise setting (involving a specific time, place, people, purpose). Where does this paragraph stand? Note what has preceded it. Luke's unique and remarkable infancy narratives (Luke 1-2) are followed by his account of the Lord's baptism, a genealogy tracing Him back to Adam (Luke 3), and a summary of His battle with Satan in the wilderness (Luke 4.1-13). All this sets the scene for the start of a public ministry of healing and teaching in Israel (4.14-15). You see, Luke's gospel presents Christ as the ideal man engaged in service to men. Our paragraph focuses in detail upon one very significant encounter between the Lord Jesus and His own townsfolk in Nazareth. How would they react to Him?

As you read the section, be attentive to the **factual information** it provides. It may help you to list the things it tells you (i) about the Saviour, (ii) about the scriptures, (iii) about the people of Nazareth (who stand as a representative sample of humanity in all its ignorance of and rebellion against God). What Paul teaches about human beings in Ephesians (2.1-3; 4.18) is here demonstrated in action. In this remarkably plain, unvarnished record of one particular visit to the local synagogue (4.16) we meet with a public reading from the Bible (4.17-19), a message based on that reading (4.20-27), and the response of the congregation (4.28-30). Observe how very down-to-earth it all is – there is nothing in the language to suggest that we

Letter No. 7 – Studying Narrative (i)

are in the imaginary fairy-tale world of myth or legend. Luke, like the rest of scripture, deals with historical 'certainty' (Luke 1.4), not with 'cunningly devised fables' (2 Pet 1.16). But although this is reliable history it is far more than mere history. Remember that no factual data is recorded in God's word without a spiritual purpose: it is there to instruct us in godliness (2 Tim 3.16-17). Therefore everything the Lord Jesus Christ does and says is a disclosure of His wonderful character; while the behaviour of the Nazarenes is a testimony to the nature of man (for, as we shall discover in a later letter, Israel is God's test-tube specimen of the entire human race).

After establishing context and collecting data comes the final step: **practical illustration**. That is to say, the pieces of information you have gathered from the passage become the basis for spiritual lessons. This is the unique value of narrative. Bible history books constitute an inspired collection of sermon illustrations, practical examples of doctrinal truth in action. Here are three examples. The writer to the Hebrews encourages his readers to meet regularly as a company of believers (Heb 10.25), but Luke actually shows us the Lord Jesus faithfully attending His local synagogue. Whereas Romans 1.2 informs us that the scriptures are 'holy' (that is, set apart from all else and to be treated accordingly), the Lord Jesus illustrates this practically in His reverent handling of a reading from the prophet Isaiah. The very way He used the Old Testament is a model of how to approach God's word – with due respect and complete confidence. Paul tells us that the Lord Jesus must have the pre-eminence in everything (Col 1.18); Luke illustrates it by describing a synagogue service where every eye was fixed on Christ (Luke 4.20). Although my first example is set in the dispensation of law under which the Saviour lived (there were of course no New Testament churches during the period of His earthly ministry), and my last is ironic in that the congregation's interest in Christ was not one of devoted worship but mere intellectual curiosity which soon turned into violent anger, I hope you can see what I mean. The idea is simply this: one-off events, locked into a space/time context, can be read as demonstrations of timeless spiritual principles.

To kick-start your own study, here are a few suggestions. **First**, note the Lord's genuine humanity. He who 'came down from heaven' (John 6.38) was 'brought up' (Luke 4.16) as a man. **Second**, the

Lord's residence in Nazareth (disdained by most orthodox Jews because it was part of Galilee, adjacent to Gentile territory) is a token of His humility (Matt 4.15; John 1.46). He who made all things and has the right to all honour condescended to live in a down-market area. Lesson: pride and arrogance should never mark those who belong to such a lowly Master (Prov 16.19; James 4.6). **Third**, the Lord's easy familiarity with the Old Testament teaches the importance of knowing our way around the word (2 Tim 3.15). Just as a young man in love will (so they tell me) pore over every tiny detail of his girl friend's letters again and again, so the believer must be well acquainted with the whole of scripture. **Fourth**, the quotation from Isaiah 61 testifies to the harmonious cooperation of each person of the Trinity in reaching out to helpless men: 'The Spirit [the Holy Spirit] of the Lord [in context, the Father] is upon me [Jehovah's perfect servant, the Son]'. Ephesians teaches that salvation is the work of Father, Son and Spirit (Eph 1.3-14): in citing Isaiah the Lord Jesus, Himself only recently publicly anointed by the Holy Spirit and announced by the Father at His baptism in the Jordan (Luke 3.21-22), endorsed this truth. **Fifth**, the quotation itself is a wonderful digest of His gracious ministry on earth, preaching good news, healing, rescuing, enlightening, liberating (4.18-19). Peter says that He 'went about doing good' (Acts 10.38), but here is a detailed summary of what that involved. **Sixth**, the quotation is a direct affirmation of the Lord's identity as long-promised Messiah: 'He hath anointed me' (4.18). Messiah, which simply means 'the anointed one', is equivalent to the New Testament title Christ. **Seventh**, the statement 'this day is this scripture fulfilled' (4.21) announced the implementation of a prediction written some 700 years before, thus underlining the infallibility of God's word. What God says will be, will be, for He alone knows the end from the beginning (Isa 46.10). **Eighth**, by intimating the fulfilment of Isaiah's words at that precise moment, Christ indicated that He personally was the theme of the Old Testament (Luke 24.27,44; John 5.46): He is the source, subject and centre of the word. **Ninth**, here is help in prophetic interpretation. The Lord pronounced the extract He read 'fulfilled', but 'closed the book' (4.20) at that point and significantly failed to read on about 'the day of vengeance of our God' (Isa 61.2). This marks the difference between His first coming in grace and His future coming in solemn judgment. **Tenth**, (and this again involves checking Isaiah 61.1-2) God's mercy extends for a 'year', while His vengeance is restricted to a 'day'. How longsuffering is our God (2 Pet 3.9)!

What we learn about the Son of God is always designed to stimulate adoration. But because He is also the perfect man and the example of everything that men ought to be, He is also a model for our behaviour. Narrative, you see, is full of dramatised doctrine and practical lessons put into action.

So keep on going. Bible study may be an investment for eternity but it will richly repay on earth all the effort you put into it. Next time, God willing, we shall look at some examples of Old Testament narrative.

Affectionately in Christ Jesus

Letter No. 8 – Studying Narrative (ii)

Dear John

Last time I wrote, I tried to suggest ways in which you can squeeze the juice out of a narrative passage from the New Testament. But we face an immediate problem when we turn to Old Testament narrative. The earthly life of the Lord Jesus and the evangelistic endeavours of His apostles recorded in Acts are of course full of straight-forward lessons for us, but all those accounts of battles, sacrifices, ceremonials, and unpronounceable kings may not seem so directly relevant. I suspect that this may be one of the reasons why many saints confine their reading to the New Testament. Let me therefore start this letter by reasserting the abiding value of the Old. Its authority is spelled out in 2 Timothy 3.16: because it is 'God-breathed' it is God's fully inspired word, just as significant as an audible voice from heaven (Deut 1.3,6). Inspiration guarantees reliability (1 Cor 10.11), for what God says cannot be untruthful (Titus 1.2). 'All these things *happened*', writes Paul. Whether we think of the supernatural blessings of the Red Sea crossing (Exo 14), the sheltering cloud, the heaven-sent manna (Exo 16), and the water-giving rock (Exo 17), or solemn judgments such as the punishment at Sinai (Exo 32.1-6,28,35), the pestilence at Shittim (Num 25.1-9) and the poisonous serpents (Num 21.1-6), we are reading factual history. Further, all these things were written 'for our admonition [*nouthesia*, a putting in mind]' (1 Cor 10.11) and 'for our learning [*didaskalia*, instruction]' (Rom 15.4), to teach us about God's ways with His people. Believers who do not study the Old Testament therefore run the risk of spiritual malnutrition.

So it is important never to forget this foundation truth: whatever God sees fit to record in His word is for His glory and our good. Let me suggest three points to keep in mind when reading Old Testament narrative. First is its basic **purpose**. It provides us with an infallible historical account of God's dealings with His people Israel, illustrations of abiding moral principles of behaviour, and typical foreviews of a coming Saviour. Its narratives are neither fiction nor legend but God-inspired truth. Yet we still have to account for all those distasteful details of savage warfare, including the annihilation of the Canaanites, and a messy sacrificial system.

This brings me to my second point, the **people** of the Old Testament. We cannot comprehend pre-Christian history until we grasp God's plan for Israel. Genesis 12 to Malachi 4 is all about God's dealings with a tiny nation, past, present and future. Why ever did He select them? As they say, how odd of God to choose the Jews! Of course, they picture His ways with believers today, but that does not exhaust their function. For a start, on the eve of entering into the Promised Land they were commissioned with the extermination of the Canaanites (Deut 20.16-18), and no stretch of exegesis can escape a mandate for genocide. To understand this, let's categorise Israel's role in the divine plan. As a nation they were to be:

1. The Channel of God's Salvation (Rom 9.4-5; John 4.22). They were chosen by God to recognise and receive the Saviour of the world. The Lord Jesus Christ, the ultimate anointed one, born under Jewish law, 'came unto his own' people Israel (Gal 4.4; John 1.11).

2. The Guardian of God's Revelation (Rom 3.2; Psa 147.19-20). They were exclusively entrusted with God's written word, which included a detailed system of laws and ordinances. Ironically, although they meticulously preserved the law by accurate copying, they failed to obey it (Acts 7.53).

3. The Testimony to God's Uniqueness (Isa 43.10; Deut 6.4). Redeemed from Egyptian slavery, they were to witness to the true God in a planet given over to polytheism and idolatry.

4. The Instrument of God's Judgment (Gen 15.16; Deut 9.4-6; Psa 149.2,5-9). As God's police-force in the world, they carried out His righteous judgments upon the wicked. Whereas believers today are 'pilgrims and strangers' on the earth, Israel was a nation under God with a commission to execute vengeance upon the ungodly. Once we allow that the sovereign Creator has the right to judge His creatures when and how He pleases, Israel's activity falls into place.

5. The Sample of God's Creation (Rom 3.19-20; Deut 8.2)   Just

Letter No. 8 – Studying Narrative (ii)

as a blood sample discloses the condition of the whole body, so Israel, entrusted with God's standards in the law yet failing to live up to those standards, proves the sinfulness of the entire human race.

Grasp the five-fold function of Israel and the Old Testament begins to make sense.

My third point is a key **principle** to remember when reading Old Testament history. While the Christian's walk, warfare and worship are spiritual, Israel's also had a physical dimension. We are to walk worthy of our high calling (Eph 4.1), but in the desert they had literally to follow the geographical guidance of the cloudy pillar (Exo 13.21-22); we fight against internal sinful desires (2 Cor 10.3-4; Col 3.5), but they battled with human enemies (Deut 20.1-4); we worship in spirit and in truth (John 4.24), but they worshipped in a God-given but worldly sanctuary (Heb 9.1). If you bear this in mind, you will be able to draw much practical encouragement from Old Testament history. So let's try an example.

Exodus 17.8-16 records one of the earliest of Israel's battles. Technical and non-devotional commentaries like that of Keil and Delitzsch will help you understand the factual data before you start drawing spiritual lessons from the story. After all, this is an unvarnished description of a supernatural victory over Israel's enemies. Never overlook the plain face-value meaning of a passage. For instance, Genesis chapter one is primarily the record of a literal six 24-hour day creation, and only secondarily a picture of spiritual salvation in Christ (2 Cor 4.6).

Having clarified the basic meaning of the passage we can look for lessons. Israel's fight was against physical foes, whereas ours is against temptations within and without, so you can easily read the contest as an **illustration of spiritual warfare**. Amalek the enemy represents everything opposed to God, perhaps especially the indwelling flesh nature (Rom 7.18; 8.8). Note especially that he attacked Israel immediately after they had drunk from the smitten rock. This is rather striking. You see, there were no battles while they were slaves in Egypt, and at the Red Sea it was God alone who saved His people from Pharaoh's pursuing army, but now Israel itself was responsible to engage in action. Lesson: the moment we get saved, spiritual warfare begins in earnest as the new believer becomes conscious of a hostile world outside and sin inside. You can learn about Amalek by using your concordance. There you will discover his origins (Gen 36.12; Deut 25.17-19). Like his ancestor Esau 'he feared not God', a reminder that the flesh in sinner or saint can never be improved and must be judged. That's why all believers experience an inner conflict (Gal 5.17) between flesh and spirit (that new principle of life received at conversion). Amalek's great opportunity was provided by Israel's stragglers (Deut 25.18), who made it easy for the enemy. Lagging behind the main company they exposed themselves to terrible danger. If we drag our heels in the Christian life or remain on the borders of assembly fellowship we shall be vulnerable to temptation and failure (Heb 10.25). Lesson: keep up with God! Until the Lord Jesus returns there will be constant war with the flesh, but each skirmish can be won by prayer (Exo 17.10) and reliance on the word (17.13).

You can also see in this story an **illustration of a prayer meeting** (Exo 17.9-12). The three men on the hill can be viewed as a company of saints at prayer, interceding on behalf of the nation. Their efforts had a decisive impact upon the course of the battle. Like believers at the assembly prayer meeting, they had a united purpose (17.10; Acts 12.12), sought a suitable place of quietness (17.10; Acts 1.13,14), enjoyed practical fellowship (17.12; Acts 1.14; 4.24), had a real impact (17.11; Acts 12.5,7), engaged in arduous spiritual effort (17.12; Col 4.12), and saw the resultant blessing (17.13; Acts 4.31). The older, spiritually mature men prayed, while the younger ones fought in the battle below. There is, you see, perfect harmony between praying *to* God and working *for* God. We can expect no blessing on the second if we omit the first.

Finally, since this is his first appearance in the Bible, you could embark upon **a study of Joshua**. Evidently Moses was training him for a future leadership role. Unlike so many who sadly love to cling on to power at all costs, Moses was primarily concerned not with his own honour but with the future needs of his people, and therefore sought to coach an able young man for coming responsibility (Exo 17.9,10,13-15). To serve God effectively demands early preparation. Joshua may have been young (Exo 33.11; 1 Tim 4.12), but he was trustworthy (Exo 17.9; Acts 16.1,2), for Moses obviously had confidence in him. He was obedient (Exo 17.10; Phil 2.20), shrewd enough to choose suitable warriors (Exo 17.9; 2 Tim 2.2), and willing

Letter No. 8 – Studying Narrative (ii)

to be taught (Exo 17.14; Matt 28.20). The lesson is clear - young men and women must cultivate spirituality right now, for it will be too late when they are older.

If we bother to put the effort into our study, there is plenty in the Old Testament to nourish our souls. Keep reading and feeding.

Affectionately in Christ Jesus

Letter No. 9 – Studying Bible Poetry

Dear John

We have already considered two distinct biblical genres: doctrinal writing (as found in the New Testament letters) and narrative (such as the gospels and the Old Testament historical books). The third kind of writing encountered in the Bible is poetry. Now all poetry involves the idea of repetition. In English we tend to think immediately of repeated sound patterns (rhyme) and repeated stress patterns (rhythm). One of my childhood favourites by Harry Graham in his deliciously sardonic *Ruthless Rhymes for Heartless Homes* goes like this:

> Father heard his children scream,
> So he threw them in the stream;
> Saying, as he drowned the third,
> 'Children should be seen, not heard'.

Terse verse but tragically poor parenting. Hebrew poetry, however, works on an entirely different principle: instead of repeated sounds or stresses it operates through repeated *ideas*. This is usually called parallelism. The thought contained in one line is reiterated (perhaps also expanded or developed) in the following line. One of the practical benefits of this is that Hebrew poetry, unlike English, can be translated into any language without losing its essential poetic quality. Rhyme and rhythm inevitably get lost in translation, but repetition of thought can be captured in any tongue. There is a wonderful universality about Hebrew song.

There are three main kinds of parallelism to watch out for in the Old Testament. First is **synonymous parallelism**. This means that an idea is repeated in different but similar words. Psalm 3.1 illustrates this for us, as David expresses to God his anxiety about the sheer number of his enemies:

> LORD, how are they increased that trouble me!
> Many *are* they that rise up against me.

Doubling the idea shows how it weighs down David's mind. One of the values of synonymous parallelism is that it often helps our interpretation of difficult Old Testament words and phrases. If there is something you cannot understand, see if the parallel line illuminates or explains it. Someone once suggested to me that Psalm 90.3 describes death in its first half but resurrection ('return') in its second. So it teaches that it is God who kills and makes alive. Well, the doctrine is of course perfectly true (see 1 Samuel 2.6 for a clear statement of it, again in a poetic context). But that is not, I think, the meaning of the psalm. A simple grasp of the principle of parallelism indicates that the two parts merely complement each other:

> Thou turnest man to destruction;
> and sayest, Return, ye children of men.

God turns men to destruction (literally, 'powder'), commanding them to 'return', not to life but to the dust from which they were made. The writer of the psalm, Moses, is echoing his own words in Genesis 3.19. Take another example. In Psalm 1.2 we learn that pleasure and meditation go hand in hand. A genuine delight in God's word is expressed in and increased by constant meditation upon its riches. The way truly to love the word is to spend time thinking seriously about it. In other words, study your Bible!

The second main form of parallelism is called **antithetical**. This sets up a sharp contrast. For example, Psalm 1.6 solemnly contrasts God's approval of the righteous with the eternal ruin of the ungodly:

> For the LORD knoweth the way of the righteous:
> But the way of the ungodly shall perish.

Incidentally, if you look up Amos 3.2 you will discover that the word 'know' here implies approval or favour rather than mere awareness. God uniquely knew Israel in the sense that He acted in grace towards it, selecting it as His chosen nation and exercising fatherly discipline when it went astray. Always remember that the Bible interprets itself.

Letter No. 9 – Studying Bible Poetry

The third kind of parallelism is called **synthetic**: this builds up a series of linked ideas. Psalm 1.1 is not just a triad of analogous thoughts; it illustrates the power of sinful company to infect us with evil habits of life.

> Blessed *is* the man that walketh not in the counsel of the ungodly,
> nor standeth in the way of sinners,
> nor sitteth in the seat of the scornful.

We learn that the blessed man (that is, the godly man) refuses to walk, or stand, or sit with those who are ungodly. That, by the way, is a powerful lesson on the value of saying 'No'! You will notice the progression: from walking through standing to sitting. It is, you see, all too easy for casual association with the people of this world (just walking along with them) to lead to a more fixed and habitual connection with them and their ways. As Paul says, 'evil communications [or companionships] corrupt good manners' (1 Cor 15.33). My best friends should be those who love the Lord.

You will be able to accumulate plenty of examples for yourself, bearing in mind that you're not restricted to the Psalms. Of course, that book alone has variety aplenty: wedding poems (45), confessions of sin (51), laments (22), prayers for help (69,70), songs of worship and praise (145), summaries of national history (105, 106). God has significantly placed at the very heart of His inspired library a collection of 150 superb lyric poems – but that is not the end of biblical poetry. In fact, about one half of the Old Testament is poetic. Not only are there five distinct books in poetic form (Job, Psalms, Proverbs, Ecclesiastes, Song of Solomon), all the prophetic books, with the interesting exception of Jonah, are written primarily in Hebrew verse. The great Old Testament foreview of Calvary in Isaiah 53 is in reality a magnificent Hebrew poem. This by no means undermines its accuracy; rather, poetry has the effect of bringing a level of powerful intensity to the written word. All this leads to the question: what is the function of poetry in the Bible?

Two things stand out. First of all, **memorability**: poetry sticks in the mind. Interestingly enough, several psalms and prophetic chapters use those alliterative techniques beloved of assembly preachers. Psalm 119 is divided into 22 sections, each devoted to a single letter of the Hebrew alphabet so that every verse in that section begins with the same letter. Even in the KJV you can see something of the effect in the stanza covering verses 65 to 72: each verse but two begins with the letter T. The psalmist uses every letter of the alphabet, all the resources of human language, to celebrate the power of God's word. The description of the virtuous woman in Proverbs 31 is alphabetical (see Newberry's margin): it is an A-Z of female godliness. Jeremiah employs a similar alphabetical technique to both measure and moderate his profound grief over the fate of Jerusalem as recorded in the book of Lamentations. But then the imagery of poetry almost always carves itself on the memory: the blessed man of Psalm 1 is like a living tree, planted, fed and fruitful, whereas the ungodly are like the wind-blown chaff – dead, useless, helpless. Hebrew seems able to express itself vividly in pictorial terms.

Secondly, poetry has the effect of adding personal **intensity** to writing. A heightened form of language captures our attention and our emotions more vividly than plain prose. David communicates deep grief by striking hyperbole: 'I am weary with my groaning; all the night make I my bed to swim; I water my couch with my tears' (Psa 6.6). Perhaps the simplest way to demonstrate the contrast between prose and verse is to compare episodes which are recorded in both forms. The creation account in Genesis chapters 1 and 2 is a prose summary of the six 24-hour days in which God made the heavens and the earth. It is very important to note that this section of the Bible is not cast in the form of Hebrew verse, for some people would love to be able to dismiss it as simply figurative or metaphorical language. It is not: it is as solid, reliable history as the remainder of the book of Genesis, and its factual accuracy is attested by scripture as a whole (Exodus 20.8-11; Mark 10.6-9). On the other hand, Psalm 104 is a poetic account of God's creative power and universal sovereignty, seeing His sustaining hand in the preservation of the world He made. A careful comparison will highlight the differences. Again, look at the prose description of the death of Sisera in Judges 4.17-22. The language is clear, unimpassioned, matter of fact, direct. But the following chapter translates cold historical narrative into all the energy of poetry that commemorates a divinely provided victory over Israel's enemies. The expanded synonymous parallelism of Deborah's Song (Judges 5.27) visualises Sisera's death at the hand of Jael with the precision of a slow motion camera:

At her feet he bowed, he fell, he lay down: at her feet he bowed, he fell: where he bowed, there he fell down dead.

Letter No. 9 – Studying Bible Poetry

We see him collapsing slowly to the earth. In reality he never fell at all, because he was slain by a tent peg while lying on the ground. But Deborah's inspired poetry creates a dramatic scene of monumental decline and fall: the proud Canaanite general is brought low.

Now, many young believers find the poetry of the Bible one of its most awkward features. This is partly because they are unfamiliar with poetry in any language, and partly because appreciation of the heartfelt agonisings of the Psalms only comes with age and experience. Poetry does not obviously relate a story, or inculcate doctrinal truth, or tell us how to behave, or spell out the future. It can and does do all those things, but in a much subtler manner than straightforward prose. When Calvin writes about the Psalms, 'I have been accustomed to call this book...*An Anatomy of all the Parts of the Soul*', he goes on to explain why: 'for there is not an emotion of which any one can be conscious that is not here represented as in a mirror'. In the fears and joys of David you will recognise the anxieties and longings of your own heart. And that can be a great comfort in distress. So do not give up on those parts of the word you find least immediately relevant. In time you will grow into them.

Affectionately in Christ Jesus

Letter No. 10 – Studying a Poem

Dear John

In my last letter I outlined some of the things you need to know when reading biblical poetry. Now it is time to examine a specific poem. Since (as I said before) the great Old Testament foreview of Calvary in Isaiah 53 is in reality a magnificent Hebrew poem, it can be treated as a specimen for analysis. Analysis can often be stimulated by asking a series of questions. I advise my students to approach any piece of literature with the aid of the following headings: subject (what is it about?), structure (what design features can you notice?), setting (what are its locations?), speakers (whose are the voices we hear?), society (who are its major people?), story (does it have a plot?), and style (what linguistic features do you see?) My students tell me that my alliteration gets rather stretched around point number five, but at least the words stick in the mind. Of course, you will not need to use them all on every occasion, but they form a handy check list.

But let us first place our poem in its context. The second great division of Isaiah's prophecy (chapters 40 – 66) is dominated by what people often call the 'Servant Songs', that is, pieces of poetry which describe a wonderful person who is able do God's will on earth without fail. Now, although Isaiah himself (Isa 20.3), and Israel as a nation (43.10; 44.1) are at times referred to as the Lord's servants, the ultimate servant of Jehovah is the Lord Jesus. Nor do we have to take this on trust. When in Acts 8.32-35 Philip gave the Ethiopian eunuch an inspired exegesis of Isaiah 53 he made it plain that the prophet was speaking not about himself but about 'Jesus'. Philip did not even say 'the Messiah' or 'Christ' (which might have allowed for the possibility that Isaiah was referring to someone who was still to come), but unambiguously identified Isaiah's servant with the man who had so recently been rejected and crucified by Israel. In other words, the passage is about the historical Jesus of Nazareth. The earlier Servant Songs describe (i) the moral character of Jehovah's perfect Servant (Isa 42.1-6), (ii) His commission (Isa 49.1-13) and (iii) His confidence in God (Isa 50.4-9). Go through them to see how they paint pen portraits of the Saviour. The fourth and final song (Isa 52.13 – 53.12) is the most memorable of all, outlining His career and triumphant sacrificial death.

Having read the passage slowly, repeatedly and carefully we can now use our seven headings. First, what is the **subject**? Well, it is emphatically Our fourth topic is the **speakers**. This unlocks some fascinating truth, because the whole poem is in fact a kind of conversation between God the Father and a future repentant Israel about the person of Christ. Just think of it: about 700 years before the Lord Jesus first came to earth we read an account of Israel's yet-to-be-uttered confession as they look back with shame to their national crime of rejecting their Messiah (John 1.11). You should be able to identify five clear sections with two distinct voices. First God speaks (52.13-15), referring to 'my servant'; then Israel (53.1-6), using the first person plural ('we') and reflecting upon Messiah's initial visit to His people; then God continues (53.7-9), alluding to Israel as 'my people'; again Israel briefly responds (53.10), this time addressing God directly ('thou') as they recognise that at the cross God made Messiah's soul 'an offering for sin'; finally God concludes the poem (53.11-12) by honouring 'my righteous servant'. God, you observe, has both the first and the last word (rather like the book of Jonah). Our God begins and finishes, for He is the Alpha and the Omega. Here we have God and man together contemplating the person and work of Christ – which is exactly what we do when we remember the Saviour at the breaking of bread. The nation of Israel will use words like this when their eyes are opened to the Lord Jesus at His glorious return (Zech 12.10). Hosea records other words they will use at the same time as they turn to God in repentance and faith (Hos 14.1-3).

Fifth, we should ponder the **society**, that is to say, the main figures of the poem: God, Israel, and Christ. We learn from Isaiah 53.10, for example, that the ultimate hand at work at Calvary was God's (Acts 2.23). Satan's malice and man's hatred were accommodated within

God's eternal purpose, for our God is gloriously sovereign. We learn from Isaiah 53.8 that the same nation which refused the Messiah is still 'my people' despite its sin (Rom 11.1). This demolishes the assertion of so-called 'replacement theology', which maintains that because of their rejection of the Lord Jesus national Israel have been permanently dislodged from God's purpose and replaced by the church. On the contrary, this entire poem anticipates their day of national restoration. But the main interest is in the person of God's Servant. Spend time and collect the details for yourself. To start you off, here's another seven S's. We learn about Christ's wise service for God (52.13; Mark 10.45), His strength as 'the arm of the Lord' (53.1; compare 51.9 and 52.10 to discover what that phrase means), His solitariness, for there was none like Him (53.2), His unique sorrows (53.3; John 11.35), His majestic silence (53.7; contrast the future dumbstruck astonishment of men in 52.15), His sacrifice (53.10, language which clearly marks Him out as the fulfilment of the whole Old Testament worship system), and His sinlessness as 'the righteous one, my servant' (53.11; B W Newton's translation). There is so much here about the Saviour to enjoy. You can usefully back it all up with New Testament parallels.

Sixth, the poem is in part a narrative because it tells a **story**. With astonishing chronological accuracy it traces (700 years in advance) the earthly life of the Lord Jesus, providing one of the great evidences for the miraculous inspiration of the Bible. We read about His manhood ('he shall grow up', 53.2; Luke 2.40), miracles ('he hath borne our griefs', 53.4a, is interpreted in Matthew 8.16-17 in relation to His sympathetic ministry of healing), rejection ('we did esteem him ... smitten of God', 53.4b; Luke 23.18), unjust trial ('taken from prison and from judgment', 53.7-8; Acts 8.33), death ('cut off out of the land of the living', 53.8; Dan 9.26), burial ('with the rich in his death', 53.9; Mark 15.42-46), resurrection (for 'he shall prolong his days', 53.10b, implies restoration to life; Matt 28.6) and exaltation ('therefore will I divide him a portion with the great', 53.12; Phil 2.9-11).

Finally, it is worth considering some aspects of **style**. Like all Hebrew poetry Isaiah 53 is full of parallelism for emphasis. The central verse (53.5) spells out with fourfold insistence the substitutionary value of Christ's death:

But he *was* wounded for our transgressions,	(a)
he was bruised for our iniquities:	(b)
the chastisement of our peace *was* upon him;	(c)
and with his stripes we are healed.	(d)

As somebody put it, this is the 'blessed exchange': He took our punishment (a and b) and gives us instead healing and peace (c and d). The New Testament equivalent is 2 Corinthians 5.21. But equally impressive is the prophet's picture language. The Servant is likened to 'a tender plant' (53.2) in His freshness and vigour, whereas sinners are 'like sheep' (53.6) in their wilful stupidity. Verse 6, by the way, is not of universal application despite the introductory 'all'. It is true only of repentant sinners, like future Israel. The 'us all' whose iniquity was laid on Him are those who in the first half of the verse unreservedly confess their sinnership ('all we'). Never forget the importance of context in determining meaning. The same holds good for Romans 5.8: the people to whom God commends His love are those who have been 'justified by faith' in verse 1. Ironically, if sinners are like sheep, so too is the Saviour – but how different! He is 'as a lamb ... a sheep' (53.7) in His submission and sacrificial death, echoing the Passover language of Exodus 12.3-5.

We can legitimately apply this wonderful prophecy to ourselves because (to quote B W Newton) 'the words of Israel's future joy form the language of our present confidence'. Having come into the good of Calvary we can see the Lord Jesus as the Servant who has done all things well. That should provide plenty of material to enrich your worship on the Lord's Day – which of course is one of the practical benefits of Bible study. Keep at it!

Affectionately in Christ Jesus

Letter No. 11 – Studying a Parable

Dear John

In my last letter I tried to demonstrate how you might profitably study a biblical poem which is simultaneously a prophecy. What I want to do now is move into one of the most difficult areas of scriptural analysis – the gospel parables. You may be surprised at the word 'difficult' – after all, isn't a parable just an earthly story with a heavenly meaning? What could be simpler? Well, yes; the Sunday School explanation has a lot going for it, not least that it foregrounds the illustrative value of the parable, with its kernel of spiritual truth. But it does not adequately prepare us for the tricky business of discovering to whom each parable is primarily applicable, nor does it caution us against the fallacy of always expecting to find a distinct meaning in every supporting detail.

Let's start with a compact **definition** from *Fausset's Bible Dictionary* (which is well worth purchasing if ever you find it). A parable is 'a placing side by side or comparing earthly truths, expressed, with heavenly truths to be understood.' So parables illustrate divine principles. Yet we often forget that their **purpose** was primarily judicial. The Saviour's early preaching was direct and straightforward. Only after Israel objected to His plain speaking did He resort to the obliqueness of parables. They were therefore a kind of punishment for those who resisted His testimony (Matt 13.10-16, 34-35), concealing truth from the unbelieving many while revealing it to the privileged few. It may also help you to bear in mind that every parable has at least three **components**: its setting, its story, and its significance. The first involves the historical circumstances which provoked its telling, the second the actual narrative, and the third the meaning. Take for example the Good Samaritan. If you read Luke 10.25-37 you will see that the parable itself (vv 30-35) is framed by a dialogue between the Lord Jesus and an expert in the Jewish religion. Luke's important signals ('tempted him...willing to justify himself') indicate that this man's approach to the Saviour was far from that of an honest inquirer. If eternal life (and you will want to ask what that meant in context) depended upon obedience to the Jewish law, what exactly was required? Unfeigned love to God and unselfish love to one's neighbour sound fine in the abstract, but what about actual practice? So the Saviour gave the example of a man in desperate need being bypassed by representatives of Judaism but rescued by a despised outsider. Having told the tale, the Lord turned to His listener with a challenging question: 'Which now of these three, thinkest thou, was neighbour unto him that fell among the thieves?' (v 36) The setting, then, was a crucial debate about the conditions for entrance into eternal life and what it meant to obey the law God gave Israel. The famous story needs no summary, but its full significance has to be worked out by the reader.

And we have some help. The chapter where the Lord starts His parable ministry includes two models of interpretation, for He expounded the Sower, and the Wheat and Tares privately to His disciples (Matthew 13.18-23,36-43). His exposition shows that a parable has a central idea around which all else revolves, and that even ancillary details can be meaningful. We must not therefore suppose that a parable is simply an expanded illustration of one spiritual truth in which the minutiae are, if I dare quote Pooh-Bah from *The Mikado*, 'merely corroborative detail, intended to give artistic verisimilitude to an otherwise bald and unconvincing narrative'. The Good Samaritan is not to be restricted to a lesson in benevolence, answering the question 'Who is my neighbour?' But nor should we assume that every tiny detail has always to be teased out and interpreted. Augustine famously allegorised everything in this parable so that (for example) the two pence given to the innkeeper came to stand for this life and the life to come. That approach gives license to the wildest flights of imagination.

Perhaps one way to avoid interpretive excess is to recall that close cousins to the New Testament parables are the Old Testament types, those marvellous foretastes of the Lord Jesus which spotlight aspects of His person and work. One of the important things to remember about them is that they all, at some point or other, break down. This

Letter No. 11 – Studying a Parable

is simply because no individual can possibly represent the Lord Jesus in His fullness. God has organised human history and His written word so that selected persons, events and ceremonies suggest features of the Saviour and His work – but they can do little more than suggest. For example, the lovely story of Abraham and Isaac in Genesis 22 involves three distinct pictures of the Saviour: Isaac stands for Him as the beloved son (v 2), the ram speaks of Him as the substitute (v 13), while conversational reference to a lamb hints at His spotlessness (v 8). Again, in 2 Samuel 9 King David's kindly treatment of Mephibosheth anticipates God's grace going out to undeserving sinners like us; but in his later dealings with Mephibosheth (2 Samuel 16,19), David is just a fallible man under stress who makes an impulsive decision which he lives to regret. My point is this. Just as we should never expect a type to conform perfectly to its spiritual counterpart, so we should avoid squeezing a parable into a preconceived doctrinal framework. I have heard gospel preachers use the Good Samaritan story and try to argue that, in allowing himself to be rescued, the traveller represents a sinner exercising faith in Christ. But the poor man was 'half dead'; he was in no condition to refuse any aid, let alone make a rational decision about practical confidence. He could neither call out for help nor make any effort to obtain it. This parable, you see, foregrounds the exercise of benevolence rather than its reception. As an illustration of God's salvation its focus is purely upon sovereign grace, *not* human responsibility. Of course, the evangelist will bring into his message the necessity of faith, but he will explain that he gets it from other scriptures. Like types, parables do not say everything that could be said. This, incidentally, suggests that we should be as wary of building doctrine on the one as on the other.

But let's now examine another familiar parable in two ways: first, to draw out its teaching, and second to highlight contrasts between the story and its significance. The passage to read is Mark 12.1-12. The story of the landlord and his tenant farmers comes from the last week of the Lord's earthly ministry, and is addressed to 'the chief priests, and the scribes, and the elders' (Mark 11.27; 12.1), who clearly recognized an unflattering portrait of themselves: 'they sought to lay hold on him, but feared the people: for they knew that he had spoken the parable against them' (12.12). It is therefore an indictment of Israel's persistent rejection of God's servants, climaxing in their slaying of the Christ. The parallels are so plain you can jot them down as you read. Here are some pointers with a few supporting scriptures, but I urge you to dig up more, remembering that each idea must always be backed up from the word. The **landlord** speaks of God, who took the initiative in giving Israel its land and privileges (Isa 43.1). The **vineyard** represents the nation, chosen to bring Him the fruit of obedient service (Psa 80.8-15; Isa 5.1-7). The **tenants** are Israel's spiritual leaders, ambitious and greedy (can you find a suitable scripture?) The **servants** are the Old Testament prophets (Jer 35.15; Matt 23.37). The landlord's one **son** makes us think of God's 'only begotten son' (John 3.16). The **judgment** anticipates God's disciplining of Israel both through the Romans in AD 70 and in the coming 'day of Jacob's trouble' (Jer 30.7; Luke 19.41-44). And while the **replacement tenants** may make us think of Gentiles coming into blessing (Rom 11.11), its prime fulfilment, I suspect, will be in a future repentant generation of Israelites (Rom 11.26).

So far the comparisons are clear. But let's now look at the parable again to observe the equally instructive contrasts. In the story the landlord 'went into a far country', so that he was at a distance from his tenants, knowing little of what was going on. But that isn't true of our God, who is eternally present, inescapable, all seeing and all knowing (Jer 23.23-24). Nothing escapes His eye. Again, in the story everything is condensed into one year, whereas God's gracious dealings with Israel cover a period of some one and a half millennia, stretching at least from the exodus to the incarnation. God's patience with His people is beyond measure (Rom 2.4). The landlord sent his final demand on the faulty supposition that 'they will reverence my son'. How little he knew the wickedness of his tenants' hearts! But God has never been under any illusions about the sinfulness of Israel or humanity as a whole (Jer 17.9). Nor did man's rejection of Christ take Him by surprise. In the parable the tenants correctly identified the heir and deliberately killed him in the expectation of gain. Did Israel's leaders recognize their Messiah? Peter and Paul (Acts 3.17;13.27) insist that they did not. This of course does not exonerate them any more than sinful blindness excuses those who today will not trust Christ. The son's death is passed over in few words: 'they took him, and killed *him*, and cast *him* out'. He had no option – in

Letter No. 11 – Studying a Parable

fact he is entirely passive and silent, the innocent, ignorant, helpless victim of malice. But the glory of the gospel is that the son of the living God knowingly and willingly took upon Himself manhood so that He might, through death, eternally deliver His people (John 10.18; Heb 2.14-15). And – mark this – He rose again.

You can see, I hope, that the parable both parallels and contrasts with the spiritual reality which lies behind it. But it is particularly worth noting the close, which shifts unexpectedly from agricultural to architectural imagery as the Lord directly challenges His audience with an Old Testament quotation: 'have ye not read this scripture; the stone which the builders rejected is become the head of the corner: this was the Lord's doing, and it is marvellous in our eyes' (Mark 12.10-11). Remember, the son has been killed – and, as far as the story is concerned, that is the end of him. But the Lord Jesus goes on to teach that the rejected son will become the exalted stone, the most significant feature in God's construction site, the pinnacle of God's programme for the universe. His miraculous resurrection and triumphant return are thus implied.

Although there is immense value in listing, cataloguing and analysing the parables one by one, they are, I suggest, always best encountered in their context. Though of wonderfully wide application and full of spiritual meat for our souls, their prime meaning is bound up with the Lord's ministry to and plans for Israel. And because we just cannot study the gospel narratives too often, when you read them again, get stuck into those parables!

Affectionately in Christ Jesus

Letter No 12 – Studying a Character

Dear John

I thought I'd conclude my little series of letters with one of the simplest and most satisfying ways of studying the word – investigating character. This is where doctrine becomes wonderfully dynamic. After all, principles are all very well in the abstract, but ordinary folk like us want to see truth worked out in daily life, and the Bible is nothing if not practical. From its very first book it hits us with a sequence of memorable figures, all of whom illustrate instantly recognisable features of genuine, sin-damaged humanity. Well known names like Abraham, Jacob, Joseph, Moses, David and Elijah are full of instruction and have been written about extensively by F B Meyer, J H Large, Hamilton Smith, A W Pink and others. Indeed, one of the best ways to learn how to study character is to see it well done by a master. But I shall concentrate now upon a minor figure who rarely gets into the limelight.

The first thing to do with **Joseph of Arimathaea** is to collect and collate the references to him in the four gospels. A good method is to use e-Sword and print the passages in parallel columns, thus:

Matthew 27	Mark 15	Luke 23	John 19
57 When the even was come, there came a rich man of Arimathaea, named Joseph, who also himself was Jesus' disciple: 58 He went to Pilate, and begged the body of Jesus. Then Pilate commanded the body to be delivered. 59 And when Joseph had taken the body, he wrapped it in a clean linen cloth,	42 And now when the even was come, because it was the preparation, that is, the day before the sabbath, 43 Joseph of Arimathaea, an honourable counsellor, which also waited for the kingdom of God, came, and went in boldly unto Pilate, and craved the body of Jesus. 44 And Pilate marvelled if he were	50 And, behold, *there was* a man named Joseph, a counsellor; *and he was* a good man, and a just: 51 (The same had not consented to the counsel and deed of them;) *he was* of Arimathaea, a city of the Jews: who also himself waited for the kingdom of God. 52 This *man* went unto Pilate, and begged the body of Jesus.	38 And after this Joseph of Arimathaea, being a disciple of Jesus, but secretly for fear of the Jews, besought Pilate that he might take away the body of Jesus: and Pilate gave *him* leave. He came therefore, and took the body of Jesus. 39 And there came also Nicodemus, which at the first came to Jesus by night, and brought a mixture of

Letter No. 12 – Studying a Character

Matthew 27	Mark 15	Luke 23	John 19
60 And laid it in his own new tomb, which he had hewn out in the rock: and he rolled a great stone to the door of the sepulchre, and departed.	already dead: and calling *unto him* the centurion, he asked him whether he had been any while dead. 45 And when he knew *it* of the centurion, he gave the body to Joseph. 46 And he bought fine linen, and took him down, and wrapped him in the linen, and laid him in a sepulchre which was hewn out of a rock, and rolled a stone unto the door of the sepulchre.	53 And he took it down, and wrapped it in linen, and laid it in a sepulchre that was hewn in stone, wherein never man before was laid.	myrrh and aloes, about an hundred pound *weight*. 40 Then took they the body of Jesus, and wound it in linen clothes with the spices, as the manner of the Jews is to bury. 41 Now in the place where he was crucified there was a garden; and in the garden a new sepulchre, wherein was never man yet laid. 42 There laid they Jesus therefore because of the Jews' preparation *day*; for the sepulchre was nigh at hand.

It then becomes easy to highlight the distinctive contributions of each evangelist to the full picture. With this information you can start assembling in your notebook an analytical study of Joseph. The alphabetical headings I am going to use may give you a template to apply to anyone in the scriptures.

First, consider his **appearance** – by which I do not mean his physical looks, in which the Bible takes little interest, as its prime focus is the heart (1 Pet 3.3-4). No, I mean his sudden emergence in the story. When, after the Saviour's arrest and crucifixion, all the disciples were still in a state of shock, and even the godly women who ministered to the Lord were unable to help, God raised up the unlikeliest of men to take care of His Son's body and arrange for its loving burial. But then our God does things like that. Out of Pharaoh's palace came the deliverer of a slave nation (Heb 11.24-26). Even though Joseph is only mentioned on this one occasion, right at the close of the Lord's earthly life, he comes out with great honour. Calvary, remember, is the touchstone of the heart: it brings out what people really are. One thief reviled the Lord Jesus; the other repented and trusted Him. The emergency makes the man.

You might then wish to investigate his **background**. We know little of his place of origin, as Arimathaea has not been conclusively identified. But we do know from Matthew that he was rich. We

Letter No. 12 – Studying a Character

sometimes get the impression that wealth *per se* is wrong. Certainly, our primary treasure should be in heaven, not in the Halifax but, as Paul teaches in 1 Timothy 6.17-19, material riches can be used down here for the Lord. Joseph illustrates his point. Further, Mark and Luke tell us he had a significant standing in society as a member of the great Jewish Sanhedrin, the ruling council of Israel. God is perfectly able to use the somebodies of this world as well as the nobodies like you and me. I think it was the Countess of Huntingdon – a devoted Christian lady of the 18th century – who said she was glad Paul wrote in 1 Corinthians 1.26 that 'not many' rather than 'not any' noble people were called by God's grace. Undoubtedly Joseph was called of God, for Matthew and John specifically tell us he was a disciple.

But what of his essential **character**, by which I mean his nature, his inner qualities? Well, he was clearly a spiritual man who 'waited for the kingdom of God' (Mark 15.43). Like Nicodemus, with whom he is associated, and like Simeon and Anna (Luke 2.25,38), he obviously knew and believed his Old Testament, because he was eagerly anticipating the establishment of the promised kingdom age (Dan 2.44; Zech 14.9; Jer 23.5). He was also 'a good man and a just' (Luke 23.50). 'Good' today may seem a fairly weak adjective, but Luke 18.19 shows how powerful it really is. He was good in his practical concern to ensure a seemly burial for the Saviour, and he was upright in that he dissented from the Sanhedrin's decision against Christ. Those who have been justified by faith ought to be just in their behaviour and good to all (Gal 6.10). And yet Joseph seems to have been a retiring man (John 19.38). His discipleship remained under wraps, perhaps because he feared the kind of ostracism suffered by others (John 9.22). But don't be too hard on him – eventually true belief will out. In any case, better to be a Joseph than a Judas who companied with the Saviour for three and a half years yet at heart was a traitor.

The **deed** for which he is best known is one of the great prophetic accomplishments in the gospels. I sometimes wonder whether in fact he was the only man in Israel who could have fulfilled Isaiah 53.9a: 'And he made his grave with the wicked [fulfilled at Calvary where the Lord was crucified between robbers], and with the rich in his death'. Did Joseph know the passage and realize that he was uniquely equipped to bring it to pass? But then of course it is God who orders all our circumstances. Of this we can be certain: the scripture cannot be broken (John 10.35). Strange, though, how people can change; in the presence of a serving maid the outspoken Peter became fearful, while the timid Joseph became courageous, entering Pilate's palace alone and 'boldly' asking for the body (Mark 15.43). It was costly to identify himself with a crucified criminal and relinquish his own memorial tomb, yet he did it.

His **example** to us is challenging. For a start it seems that it stirred another quiet disciple, Nicodemus, into action (John 19.39). How often the good example of one believer encourages others to follow his lead. That, I think, was the case with Daniel and his three young friends in Babylon (Dan 1.8-12). Joseph's official request also bore witness to Pilate who, as a result, became aware of the astonishingly early death of the Lord Jesus (Mark 15.44). It is, you see, worth noting that Joseph did not attempt to remove the body furtively, under cover of darkness; rather, he went through the correct channels, showing all respect to the civil powers (Rom 13.1). His action demonstrated real devotion to the Saviour, providing Him with a princely burial though the mourners were few. We should never judge a man by the size of his funeral. And, like a godly Jew, he made sure he observed Sabbath law (John 19.42). Joseph did the right thing in the right way.

My final point is **fellowship**. Although it seems initially that Joseph stood alone, God raised up another to join him. Joseph and Nicodemus had a number of things in common – for a start, they were both materially affluent and socially reputable – but it was love for Christ which truly united them. Their aim was to honour a Saviour who had been rejected by men. Each of them, you will note, had a distinct role: Joseph provided the grave clothes and the tomb, Nicodemus the expensive spices. Yet each worked in glad harmony with the other. Now that's a lovely picture of what things ought to be like in our local assemblies – different people working together in happy concord for the glory of Christ Jesus.

Not much is said about Joseph of Arimathaea but what *is* said is, like all the word, 'profitable for doctrine, for reproof, for correction, for instruction in righteousness' (2 Tim 3.16). May these little hints encourage you to dig deep, dig diligently and dig daily into the rich, inexhaustible mine of God's word. You'll never regret it!

God bless and lots of love in Christ Jesus.